Amanda Kane, 18   Lisa Meyer, 33

*My niece Amanda and I have made some great
memories while writing Quotes for Kids.
We've discovered we have what it takes to write a book:
openness, respect, humor and lots of love.*

Health, and happiness to you and all you love.

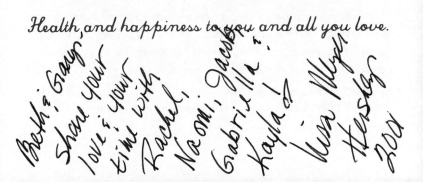

What teachers are saying about Quotes for Kids:

"A much-needed review of the virtues which develop character and integrity, this publication is thoughtfully designed with youth in mind. Carefully selected quotations provide enrichment for the reader."

MRS. NANCY HOFF
5th Grade Teacher, 25 years teaching experience.

"Hopefully, these words can be read and absorbed by a generation much in need of honor, integrity and ethical behavior."

MR. JOE SAILE
7th Grade English Teacher, 33 years teaching experience.

"I feel this book should be in every school, it would be an interesting teaching tool for families and students. Quotes for Kids really makes you think about your role in life."

DOC. BENDER
10th Grade Biology Teacher, 35 years teaching experience.

"Lisa's book has the power to inspire our kids to find meaning and get out of life what really matters. As a life-long friend I know the sincerity and depth that has gone into its contents and...all of it really matters."

WANDA WAGNER-SMITH
Phys. Ed. Teacher/Trainer, 25 years teaching experience.

Quotes for Kids

Today's Interpretations of Timeless Quotes Designed to Nurture the Young Spirit

By Lisa Meyer
Illustrated by Dan Holt, Ph.D.

P.O. Box 764 ♦ Hershey, PA 17033

Reach Press, Hershey, Pennsylvania 17033

First Edition - *Second Printing*

Printed in the United States of America.
Printed on acid-free paper.

All correspondence and inquiries should be directed to
Reach Press, P.O. Box 764, Hershey, PA 17033.

082
MEY © 1998 Meyer, Lisa C., 1964

Quotes for kids : today's interpretations of timeless quotes designed to nurture the young spirit / by Lisa Meyer; Illustrated by Dan Holt, Ph.D. - Hershey, PA : Reach Press, © 1998.

160p. : ill.. ; 18.5 cm.
Includes index

Summary: A collection of classic quotes with modern interpretations for adolescents.

Library of Congress Catalog# 97-069588

ISBN 0-9660148-0-4

1. Quotations, English - Juvenile literature 2. Wit and humor, Juvenile 3. Philosophy - Juvenile literature 1. Holt, Dan, ill. II. Title

PN6081   082_dc21

Provided in cooperation with Unique Books, Inc.

Page design and layout by Amy Fake, Graphic Artist

Acknowledgements

To my beautiful niece Amanda, what a joy watching you grow!

To Mary Beth Blegen, although we've never previously met, I believed we had to share some of the same visions; I simply asked you to write the foreword and you did. Recognizing the impact this book could have on our kids, you took the time to write a foreword that speaks on behalf of kids and sends a powerful message to their parents.

To my past teachers, thank you for all of the years of dedication, your belief in youth and your confidence in me.

Where would we be without friends? To Bonnie Kaye, Barbara E., Jane, Vicki, Danene, Wanda, Shelley, Holly, Brenda, I am blessed.

To Amy Fake, Richard Schaeffer, Sharon Castlen, Dan Holt.

Special thanks to Scott Miller of DISC, for your talents.

To my Aunt Sandie and Aunt Arlene for all your love and expressions of kindness. To my mom, Nancy, and sisters Kim, Donna, Joey, and Rose, for giving me strength in many different ways.

To Jody, you have evoked some of my most sincere thoughts.

In the first week of September 1997 we have lost two of the greatest humanitarians of our time, Lady Diana Spencer and Mother Teresa. How and where do we begin to carry the torch that they have passed down to us? Perhaps if we begin by adding light to the lives of the people closest to us, just as they have, we will gain the strength to reach out to the rest of the world, a little at a time.

In memory of my Dad.
He believed I could fly...and now I do too.

Table of Contents

*Everybody today seems to be in such a terrible rush,
anxious for greater developments and greater riches
and so on, so that children have very little time for their
parents. Parents have very little time for each other,
and in the home begins the disruption of the peace
of the world.*

MOTHER TERESA OF CALCUTTA
*(1910-1997) Albanian-born Roman Catholic nun.
Awarded Nobel Peace Prize 1979*
*Also awarded America's highest honor,
the Presidential Medal of Freedom 1985*

Foreword

For 30 years I taught school in Worthington, Minnesota, a town of 10,000 on the prairies of Minnesota. I taught history, writing and humanities, but more importantly, I taught kids. Kids of all backgrounds, of all economic levels and of all intelligence levels. Wonderful kids who came to school looking for help in growing up. They learned in many ways. In the classroom. In the gym. In the theater. On the football field.

The biggest single need those kids have is to be heard. They need to be heard by parents, by teachers, by friends and by other adults. They have so much going on in their heads and hearts which is so very important. If you were 16 today and nobody was listening to you, how would you come to any understanding of who you are and where you fit in today's world? They are crying out to be heard. Crying in a variety of ways. But crying loudly.

Our kids are important. I believe that we know that, but we don't always want to take the time that they demand. To know and listen to a kid takes moments and hours and days. The listening can't be selective. The listening must go on and on and on.

Kids also need to come to their own sense of importance. That process is long and hard. It takes help from the outside, but it also takes much work from the inside. Kids need encouragement from many sources.

It is my hope that Lisa's book will provide a bit of encouragement to kids and offer them a moment of reflection.

Kids are worth every ounce of our investment. We must listen to them and nurture them.

Mary Beth Blegen

Mary Beth Blegen
1996 National Teacher of the Year

Introduction

Why have I written this book? It is because I've met far too many young people who did not have the kind of father I had. Someone who could teach them the fundamentals of life. Although he is no longer here, I believe parts of him still live on in me, and I can share his wisdom through this book. Every time I see young eyes I want to show them love. I want them to know what it means to make something from nothing, to turn the negative into a positive, and to stimulate him or her into realizing their personal best. That's what the circle of life is all about. This book is the start of my part in making the world a better place.

I believe the young lives that we bring into this world are capable of understanding far more than what we adults give them credit for. This collection of timeless quotes shared with your special young adult will help to develop higher thinking about the things that matter most in life.

While writing this book and developing my interpretations of each quote, it became increasingly clear to me that these great philosophers had the same basic messages:

🐾 Positive thoughts create positive thinking, and a positive mind is the first step in reaching our personal best.

🐾 The only true limitations are the ones we set for ourselves.

🐾 It is far better to give than to receive.

🐾 The most valuable things in life are free.

🐾 The most precious gifts that we have to give are our time and our love.

These basic virtues have been a part of our humanity since the beginning of time: goodness is goodness, honesty is honesty, truth is truth. They haven't changed. I have come to learn these truths and to accept what it took for me to realize them. It's because of this that I have tried to express our great philosophers' concepts in such a way that it becomes clear to all who read them. Each word and illustration have been intended to stimulate higher thinking and create understanding.

Life's valuable lessons are most times brutal and a higher understanding is the life preserver that will keep one's spirit afloat. Ralph Waldo Emerson said: "All that Adam had, all that Caesar could, you have and can do...Build, therefore your own world." Quotes for Kids is a tool to help someone you love to build their world.

In my heart of hearts I want all people to know these strengths. The key is to start learning them as early in your life as you can. That's why this book is entitled Quotes for Kids. I want us all to feel empowered, and to have a full and happy life. Just as looking at favorite pictures again and again can uncover something new, reading this book again and again may reveal something you haven't seen before. Share it and your time with someone you love.

Lisa Meyer

Lisa Meyer

Attitude

Watch your thoughts; they become words.
Watch your words; they become your actions.
Watch your actions; they become your habits.
Watch your habits; they become character.
Watch your character; it becomes your destiny.

AUTHOR UNKNOWN

As he thinketh in his heart, so is he.

PROVERBS 23: 7

All that Adam had, all that Caesar could, you have and can do...build, therefore, your own world.

RALPH WALDO EMERSON
(1803-1882) American. Essayist, Poet, Philosopher

There have been and still are many great people in this world. But they are no greater than you.

You have what it takes to do incredible things. GO FOR IT!

All the world's a stage, and all the men and women in it are merely players. They have their exits and their entrances; and one man in his time plays many parts.

SHAKESPEARE
(1564-1616) English. Poet, Playwright

The world is a place to show what you can do. We all have a place in it. It's the circle of life. It never ends.

Act your part with honor.

EPICTETUS
(55?-135?) Greek. Philosopher

You are not only good to yourself, but the cause of goodness in others.

SOCRATES
(470?-399? BC) Greek. Philosopher

       If you are an OK basketball player and you start hanging around someone who plays better than you, you start to learn from watching. Your game will get better and better.

       Don't stop here - pull the good stuff out of everyone who is around you! Be someone the other kids can learn from and look up to. Kids need good examples. They are watching!

Children have more need of models than of critics.

JOSEPH JOUBERT
(1754-1824) French. Moralist

He is only bright that shines by himself.

GEORGE HERBERT
(1593-1633) English. Poet

If you wait until other people want to do the things you want to do you could wait forever. And if you depend on other people too much, most times you'll be disappointed.

If you and your friends are on the soccer team and you really want to do something different like tennis and your friends don't, do it without them. You'll probably make new friends and you might even like it more than soccer.

Hitch your wagon to a star. Let us not fag in paltry works which serve our pot and bag alone. Let us not lie or steal. No god will help. We shall find all their teams going the other way; every god will leave us. Work rather for those interests which the divinities honor and promote - justice, love, freedom, knowledge, utility.

RALPH WALDO EMERSON
(1803-1882) American. Essayist, Poet

The universe - it's a big one. Explore it! Make your star shine! Think about Mother Teresa; she started her legacy just by helping poor children in the streets. In her lifetime she opened hundreds of centers around the world for the poor and the sick. It was her faith, her unselfish love, and her commitment to helping others that made her one of the most well-known, and highly respected women in history. I know what you're thinking, "I'm not Mother Teresa!", and you don't think you could ever do what she did. But you know what... I'll bet she didn't think so either.

We can do no great things; only small things with great love.

MOTHER TERESA
(1910-1997) Albanian. Nun, Missionary, Noble Peace Prize, Presidential Medal of Freedom

Nothing on earth can stop the man with the right mental attitude from achieving his goals; nothing on earth can help the man with the wrong mental attitude.

W.W. ZIEGE
(unavailable)

Have you heard people say, "You are what you eat?" Well I'll bet you haven't heard this one, "You are what you think." You will become what you think about, so keep the good thoughts in your head and the bad ones out. That's what it's all about! (Kinda like the hokie pokie.)

A great man by the name of Samuel Joseph once said:
When I die, God will not ask me, "Why were you not
Moses?" When I die, God will ask me,
"Why were you not Samuel?"

UNKNOWN

Try not to compare yourself to others, you don't have to follow the crowd.

Be what you choose to be, not what others tell you they think you should be. Yes!

Think not those faithful who praise all thy words and actions; but those who kindly reprove thy faults.

SOCRATES
(470?-399? BC) Greek. Philosopher

In gymnastics, like all sports, there is a coach. When the young gymnast lands a great cartwheel the coach usually says, "Good job." (Encouragement is important.) But, if the gymnast is ever going to learn how to do a round-off, back handspring, double back somersault, with a full twist, the coach has to gently show her what she is doing wrong to help her become a better athlete.

Without the coaching the cartwheel is as good as it's ever gonna get. You won't reach your fullest potential.

Search for great coaches and teachers in your life, and try to be a great coach/teacher yourself (not a royal know-it-all).

If a man has not a good reason for doing something,
he has one good reason for letting it alone.

SIR WALTER SCOTT
(1771-1832) Scottish. Novelist, Poet

If you can't find a good reason for doing
something, well then, I guess you shouldn't do it!
It kind of goes along with if you don't have
anything nice to say don't say anything at all.

In the central place of every heart there is a recording chamber; so long as it receives messages of beauty, hope, cheer, and courage, so long are you young. When the wires are all down and your heart is covered with the snows of pessimism and the ice of cynicism, then only are you grown old.

DOUGLAS MACARTHUR
(1880-1964) American. General

    No matter how old we get we still need to feel love and encouragement. And when we start to feel unloved or discouraged our lives begin to feel empty and alone. Our whole attitude changes and so does our life.

thoughts....

Beauty

*Was she so loved because her eyes were
so beautiful or were her eyes so beautiful
because she was so loved?*

ANZIA YEZIERSKA
(1885-1970) American. Author

Beauty without grace is the hook without the bait.
Beauty, without expression, tires.

RALPH WALDO EMERSON
(1803-1882) American. Essayist, Poet, Philosopher

So, if you are fishing and all you have
is the hook and not the bait, you won't
catch too many fish (at least not the smart
ones). All you really have is an empty hook.
Physical beauty is a lot like this, it's just there
with nothing to back it up.

Here's the goal...

Show the stuff that counts. Show
your beauty that comes from the inside. Always
be kind, generous and happy. Because if you
just show the hook (physical beauty) the
friends you catch may not be the ones you keep.
Remember it was the not-so-smart fish that bit
at the empty hook in the first place.

So don't just use the hook or just
the hook and the bait, use your whole rod!

Beauty is a short lived reign.

SOCRATES
(470?-399? BC) Greek. Philosopher

Good looks won't get you too far for too long. Have you ever met someone who you thought was really gorgeous but after you got to know this person you realized they were a real jerk? Now this person is not so gorgeous. (As a matter of fact they may be down right ugly.) What really makes a person pretty is what is on the inside, not just what's on the outside.

I can still hear my Dad's voice saying to me "pretty is as pretty does." Think about it. Hey, maybe Forrest Gump and I are distant cousins!

I pray thee, O God, that I may be beautiful within.

SOCRATES
(470?-399? BC) Greek. Philosopher

Physical beauty is a nice thing to have but it is not what's important. What is important is to be a good person. Always try to do the right thing, be honest with yourself and others. And always keep positive thoughts in your head.

If you do this you will have a beauty all your own, one that the best looking kid in school may never get.

Personal beauty is a greater recommendation than any letter of introduction.

ARISTOTLE
(384-322 BC) Greek. Author, Philosopher

When you have inner beauty you don't need a letter of introduction, because it shows. It shows in the way you talk, the way you walk and in the way you carry yourself. Your beauty shows in the way that you treat other people, in what you say to them and how you say it.

Strive to be prettier on the inside than you are on the outside!

*Though we travel the world over to find the beautiful,
we must carry it with us or we will find it not.*

RALPH WALDO EMERSON
(1803-1882) American. Essayist, Poet

If you don't know what is beautiful about
yourself, you will not see all the beautiful things
around you or the goodness in others.

Character

*Keep away from people who try to belittle your
ambitions. Small people always do that,
but the really great make you feel
that you, too, can become great.*

MARK TWAIN
(1835-1910) American. Writer, Humorist,

*No one can make you feel inferior
without your consent.*

ELEANOR ROOSEVELT
(1884-1962) American. First Lady, Social Reformer

Only in winter can you tell which trees are truly green.
Only when the winds of adversity blow can
you tell whether an individual or a country
has courage and steadfastness.

JOHN F. KENNEDY
(1917-1963) American. The 35th President of the United States

Beauty is in the eye of the beholder. Nature and books belong to the eyes that can see them. It depends on the mood of the man, whether he shall see the sunset or the fine poem. There are always sunsets, and there is always genius; but only a few hours so serene that we can relish nature or criticism.

RALPH WALDO EMERSON
(1803-1882) American. Essayist, Poet, Philosopher

If you look for beauty and goodness you will find it wherever you go. I was walking out of the grocery store one day and waiting for me was one of the most spectacular sunsets I have ever seen in my life. I counted two other people who took the time to stop and enjoy its beauty. We knew that in less than twenty minutes it would be gone, and we didn't want to miss it. Sadly, the other people didn't see it, they didn't even know it was there!

Some of the most nourishing moments are given to us as gifts, like a sunset. But, you have to stop and see it while it's in the sky, not when you have the time to stop and watch it. It's not gonna wait for you!

Just as nature can improve our lives so can criticism. If someone you respect and trust is willing to tell you something about yourself to help you be a better person, and not to hurt you, listen. Be grateful to that person, because they are showing you that they care about you, and they don't want to see you keep making the same mistakes. It's not as hard as it sounds, and it might take a little while. You can do it. Ask questions like, "Do I really do that? When did I do that? Why do you think that? What can I do differently next time?" Think about what the person is saying, and make sure they are being honest with you. Then you can decide for yourself if you need to change. Ask another person you trust and respect. It's good to get a second opinion.

My close friends have told me some things about myself that I really needed to hear. At the time, I wasn't so sure, but now I am so thankful they've told me. It has made me a much better person. I've grown from it, and our friendships have grown closer too!

The history of every country begins in the heart of a man or a woman.

WILLA CATHER
(1873-1947)   American. Writer

We are the backbone of our country. What we feel in our hearts is what we will pass down to the next generation, one family at a time. What you believe in, what you do and what you say are important.

These are the things that will make us or break us in the future. We're all in this together. What do you want to pass down to the next generation of Americans?

This above all: to thine ownself be true, And it must follow, as the night the day, Thou canst not then be false to any man.

WILLIAM SHAKESPEARE
(1564-1616)   English. Poet, Playwright

Simply, be true to yourself. Don't let other people mold you into their expectations. Find yourself. Only then can you be true to others.
Live the life you dream of.

So it is, and such is life. The cat's away, the mice they play.

CHARLES JOHN HUFFMAN DICKENS
(1812-1870) English. Author, Dramatist

Sometimes when the "boss" is away, everybody wants to play.

Be the one to do the right thing. Do a good job, not just for your boss, but for yourself too! It makes you feel proud when you know you've done your best!

Our characters are the result of our conduct.

ARISTOTLE
(384-322 BC) Greek. Author, Philosopher

We are not talking cartoon characters here. We are talking about our character, the stuff we're made of. What makes us who and what we are and all we want to be.

Our conduct is the way we act, it shows the person we are. We show what we know. Now be careful not to judge a person by only one thing they do or say. It takes a lot of different thoughts and ideals to make up a person's character. So look at some other people's characters, learn from them. Put a lot of thought and effort into your own personal character.

Communicating

Conversation is an art in which a man has
all mankind for his competitors, for it is that
which
all are practicing every day while they live.

RALPH WALDO EMERSON
(1803-1882) American. Essayist, Poet, Philosopher

Great conversation...requires an absolute
running of two souls into one.

RALPH WALDO EMERSON
(1803-1882) American. Essayist, Poet, Philosopher

Communicating

The way a person communicates is one of the ways we express who we are. Think about and be very careful what you say and how you say it. Make sure you mean what you say; and be sure the other person really understands what you're saying.

Many times we think the other person understands what we are saying, but they don't. The message that was sent was not the message received. This is when disaster hits. And when the communication lines are not open (that means someone doesn't want to talk or listen) anything the other person says will just make things worse. When this happens give the other person some time to think things through. Let them know you are willing to listen when they are ready to talk. You've got to talk, because you never really know what a person is thinking and feeling until they tell you, and sometimes they don't even know themselves.

If you are the one who is upset tell the other person exactly what they did, how it made you feel, and what they should do differently the next time. Don't attack the person by calling them a "knuckle-head." Calmly tell them how you feel, so the two of you can work things out.

Sometimes we don't need to use words to communicate. I was visiting a woman in a nursing home. Sadly, she can best be described as her daughter says, a "vegetable." She didn't know her own name and she couldn't talk. One warm summer evening I wheeled her outside and began reading the manuscript of this book to her. She kept gesturing to me; she clearly wanted something, but what? I paid close attention to her. It didn't take me long to realize this lady whom I had only met the week before just wanted me to hold her. I gave her a big hug. And then I looked directly at her face and I saw a beautiful warm smile. Hugs cost nothing, take little effort, and they express so much.

I hope I never forget the smile on Jackie's face that day. At that moment I knew there was more to say in this chapter. I had to tell you that people communicate in all types of ways, you just have to learn how to listen and how to respond to them. Sometimes words are only necessary when love is gone.

Wise men talk because they have something to say;
fools because they would like to say something.

PLATO
(Circa 428-c. 347 BC) Greek. Philosopher

Plato

    You know it's true. How many times have you heard someone talking and you thought to yourself, "What is this person trying to say?" You wouldn't want this to be said about you, would you? When you talk say something worth saying. Some people just blah, blah, blah. Why do they do this? Just to hear themselves talk? They're not really saying anything that's worth listening to.

    Watch the people you are talking to. The way people respond tells you if they are interested in what you are saying, or that they really wish you would just be quiet.

    If someone doesn't want to listen to you, then you are wasting your breath, because they won't hear a thing you say. Honest! Aren't you the same way?

Courage is what it takes to stand up and speak:
courage is also what it takes to sit down and listen.

UNKNOWN

You've got to know when to talk and when to listen. Because if you say something you didn't mean and then apologize for it later, even if the other person says they forgive you, they usually never forget it.

Oh be careful little mouth what you say!

The difference between the right word and the
almost right word is really a large matter - it's
the difference between lightning and the lightning bug.

MARK TWAIN
(1835-1910) American. Writer, Humorist

There is a huge difference between lightning
and the lightning bug. So, if you use the word "or,"
but you really meant to use
the word "and," that makes
a difference. Choose
your words
carefully, be
direct and to
the point.

A man who uses a great many words to express his meaning is like a bad marksman who instead of aiming a single stone at an object takes up a handful and throws at it in hopes he may hit.

SAMUEL JOHNSON
(1709-1784) English. Writer, Lexicographer (helps to write dictionaries)

Abraham Lincoln's famous Gettysburg Address was written by using 28% multi-syllable words and 72% single syllable words. So here's proof that a powerful message can be sent in a clear and concise way without all the extra flash.

Simple words like faith, hope, joy, and love are the most powerful; they have a meaning everybody can understand and relate to.

The golden rule is do unto others as you would have them do unto you.

The platinum rule is treat people the way they want to be treated.

How can you tell the way people want to be treated you ask? It's simple, it's the same way they're treating you!

One of the things I learned when I was a waitress was how to read people. I knew within seconds after taking their order if I should call them Mr. and Mrs. Customer, or if I could call them by their first names, Joe and Jody. It just takes a little effort to see if someone is real stiff and formal, or if they are more on the casual side, and then go from there.

Sometimes people are short with you and it may seem like they are almost being rude. But, if you play along with them, they usually enjoy it and it makes them laugh. (Most of my family does this.) I have met some people who were mean to me. I chose not to treat them the way they've treated me. Now, I just stay away from them. I don't like to be mean. It's just not me.

The bitterest tears shed over graves are for words left unsaid and deeds left undone.

HARRIET BEECHER STOWE
(1811-1896) American. Writer, Abolitionist

Do the little extra things that show someone you care. Then if for some reason they're not in your life anymore, you'll be glad you didn't miss those chances. Do what you can while you can. Take the time to make a memory! My sister Donna says memories are little pieces of happiness we carry with us inside. I agree.

thoughts....

Determination

Constant dripping hollows out a stone.

LUCRETIUS
(circa 99-55 BC) Roman. Poet

Perfection is attained by slow degrees;
it requires the hand of time.

FRANCOIS MARIE AROUET VOLTAIRE
(1694-1778) French. Writer, Philosopher

There is no such thing as a great talent
without great will-power.

HONORÉ DE BALZAC
(1799-1850) French. Writer, Novelist

The rung of a ladder was never meant to rest upon,
but only to hold a man's foot long enough to enable
him to put the other somewhat higher.

THOMAS HENRY HUXLEY
(1825-1895) British. Biologist

*Dissatisfaction with the world in which we live and
determination to realize one that shall be better,
are the prevailing characteristics of the modern spirit.*

GOLDSWORTHY LOWES DICKINSON
(1862-1932) English. Historian, Essayist, Lecturer

If you know something is wrong be
determined to change it. This is the kind of spirit
that has made our country so great.

It wasn't very long ago when women did not
have the right to vote. Instead of just accepting this,
women fought for this right until they got it.

This wouldn't have happened if they weren't
determined to fight for what they believed in.

There was never a time in my youth, no matter how dark and discouraging the days might be, when one resolve did not continually remind me, and that was a determination to secure an education at any cost.

BOOKER T. WASHINGTON
(1856-1915) American. Educator, Author

No matter how hard the day can get, or how tough things seem to be at the time, don't give up! Things usually have a way of working out.

It was worth it then and it is worth it now. Education is power! Be determined and stick with it! You can do it; all you need to do is try. Never stop learning no matter how old you get. Education will get you everywhere!

*Press on: Nothing in the world can take the place of
perseverance. Talent will not; nothing is more common
than unsuccessful men with talent. Genius will not;
unrewarded genius is almost a proverb. Education will
not; the world is full of educated derelicts. Persistence
and determination alone are omnipotent.*

CALVIN COOLIDGE
(1872-1933) American. The 30th President of the United States

There are whole bunches of people who have a
good education, are real smart, and even have talent
but, they don't have the best job that they could get.
Why? Maybe it's because they quit too soon, and
didn't stick with it long enough to see what they can
do. Or maybe it's because they need to change their
attitude.

I know some very successful business people
who have average intelligence, but they are very
persistent, hard working, and they know how to make
things happen. What do they get for all this effort?
You guessed it. They get the "big bucks!"

Consider the postage stamp my son. Its usefulness consists of its ability to stick to one thing until it gets there.

ANONYMOUS

Think about how simple the postage stamp is. I mean you just put the little guy on the envelope and it stays there until its job is done. It never whines about being too hot or too cold and it doesn't give up. This seems really simple but think about it: this little, tiny, eensy-weensy stamp can travel all the way from here to China. So whatcha think about that?!

If your determination is fixed, I do not counsel you to despair. Few things are impossible to diligence and skill. Great works are performed not by strength, but perseverance.

SAMUEL JOHNSON
(1709-1784) English. Critic, Lexicographer, (helps to make dictionaries)

If you have determination you are on the right track. You can get what it takes to reach your goals.

The one thing that all the great people in the world have had in common is persistence. They did not quit when things got a little tough because they knew they could do whatever it took to get the job done. And they did!

We can do anything if we stick to it long enough.

HELEN KELLER
(1880-1968) American. Author, Lecturer

When the going gets tough, the tough get going.

People do not lack strength, they lack will.

VICTOR HUGO
(1802-1885) French. Poet, Novelist, Playwright

When you have the will, the strength follows.
You gain confidence; you know you can do whatever
you set your mind to do.

If you have the will to learn
how to swim then you will learn.
You have to begin small and work your way up.
First, you start out being a guppy swimming around
in a little, inky, dinky fishbowl but soon, you'll get to
swim in the seemingly endless ocean with the even
bigger fish.

You've got to have the will! You've got to want to!

They build too low who build beneath the skies.
An inscription on a building in Washington D C.

Why build a clubhouse when you can build a
castle? Start low, aim high! Your determination will
take you there!

Emotions

What I know about emotions is that you cannot trust them, for they will tell you one thing one minute and another the next. Learn to control your emotions before they control you. Let your emotions guide you to where your destiny lies; do not allow them to navigate the whole journey.

LISA MEYER

Emotions

Human emotions are tricky, and you can't trust them. Have you ever noticed that one minute you feel excited about something and the next minute you are not so sure about it. Or what about the times you were really angry about something and now you can laugh about it. Human emotions are in us to trigger an action, but you have to control what you do with them. If you don't, your emotions will control you.

Say someone has said something nasty to you, immediately you feel hurt, but now you have a decision to make. You can either say something mean back to them (which most times just makes things worse), or you can make the decision not to get upset. You see, people do not get you angry, you let them make you angry. It's true. So don't give them that power. I believe that not too many things in this world are worth getting upset over. There are going to be times in life when you must be forceful, but not too many.

You remember this one... "Sticks and stones may break my bones, but words will never harm me." Stand firm for what you believe in; you get a lot of strength when you know that what's in your own heart is pure.

When you share your emotions with someone else be sure you are prepared to accept what they might do with them. Because some people may stomp on them and they won't care what you are feeling, while others may be understanding and concerned.

The people who don't care about what you are feeling are usually the kinds of people you don't want to hang around with anyway. Stay away from them, and surround yourself with people who are loving and supportive.

And when it's your turn to be the one to listen, make sure you are truly listening, and not just sitting there silently, waiting for your turn to speak. Because if you do not listen how can you ever begin to understand what the other person is saying?

So you are kind of sticking your neck out when you share your emotions but if you don't you will never have a close relationship with anyone. This is one of the things that brings people closer together. It's a way of opening up so you can give love and get it.

*Anybody can become angry-that is easy; but to be angry
with the right person, and to the right degree, and at the
right time, and for the right purpose, and in the right
way-that is not within everybody's power and is not easy.*

ARISTOTLE
(384-322 BC) Greek. Author, Philosopher

So now you know that getting mad is a little
more complicated than you thought. Sometimes the
only thing some people understand is anger. They
don't get what you are trying to tell them unless you
are shouting at them. This is not a good thing, but it
is true.

So it's OK to get angry at the right things and
with the right people (don't shoot the messenger) in a
way that's reasonable and for a certain amount of
time. Don't hold a grudge or stay mad forever, you
are only hurting yourself when you do. Remember that
you have control of your emotions, not anyone else. If
it's not worth getting upset over, don't!

Don't permit yourself to show temper. Always remember that if you are right you can afford to keep your temper, and if you are wrong you cannot afford to lose it.

J. REYNOLDS
(unavailable)

Did you ever feel like a jerk when you got mad at someone and said things you didn't mean? I know I have. This does not have to happen to you anymore (well a lot less anyway).

Remember you have control of this and no one can make you angry unless you let them. So the next time your brother or sister goes in your room and you don't want them in there, don't freak and get mad. It'll take some practice. You can do it!

We could never learn to be brave and patient,
if there were only joy in the world.

HELEN KELLER
(1880-1968) American. Author, Lecturer

Why do we need to learn how to be brave and patient you ask? Because when you are brave you can face what is ahead of you and you know you have what it takes to handle it. When you have patience you don't lose your temper or your dignity. You know that a little time helps to make a confusing situation easier to understand. Things usually have a way of working out.

One of the reasons life can't be filled only with joy is because we would never appreciate all the good things in life. How many blessings do you take for granted everyday? Think about it!

Forgiveness

It is only when we know pure love that we are able to forgive; and when we release the pain it brings, the warm nourishing sunlight can come in.

LISA MEYER

Forgiveness

Sometimes we hurt another person and we don't even know it. We know we are upset, and most times the other person is hurt and upset too. The closer you are to someone the more it hurts when they do something you don't like. Forgiving someone may seem really hard. But it's nothing compared to how you will feel if you do not forgive.

Hate and anger are poisons. If you don't forgive other people, these poisons (feelings of hate and anger) will get stronger and stronger. Soon you will be filled with so much hate and anger you will hate most everybody and everything. It will ruin your life. The bad thing is you won't even know it is happening!

Forgiveness does not mean you accept or agree with what the other person has done. It just means letting go of the hate and anger. It is one of those things in life that is real hard to do. And it is one of those things in life that you must do.

If you can forgive someone for a "little thing" like hurting your feelings, then when life hits you with the "big things" like having to forgive the person who has hurt someone you love, you will be able to. Forgiveness brings a consoling, warming peace.

God has opened my heart with forgiveness for the person who took my father's life. I have peace.

Habit

When we have practiced good actions awhile they become easy; when they are easy we take pleasure in them; when they please us we do them frequently; and then, by frequency of act they grow into habit.

TILLOTSON
(1630-1694) English. Prelate, Religious Leader

Habit is either the best of servants, or the worst of masters.

EMMONS
(unavailable)

A good habit can be like a best friend. A bad habit can be your worst enemy. Good habits start with brushing your teeth twice a day. And then they grow into really good habits like getting up earlier, working a little later to get a job finished, or taking really good care of yourself.

Habits lay the foundation of success or failure, good or evil, and make the difference between a happy, full life and an unproductive one. Start today and instill good habits in yourself.

We first make our habits, and then our habits make us.

JOHN DRYDEN
(1631-1700) English. Poet, Dramatist, Critic

This is why it is so important to have good habits, because they show who you are.

If you make it a habit to always try to do your best, you will be your best. If you don't, you won't!

All our knowledge is symbolic.

JOHANN WOLFGANG VON GOETHE
(1749-1832) German. Poet, Dramatist, Author

We show what we know. It's a symbol of us, just like our habits are.

We are what we repeatedly do. Excellence, then is not an act but a habit.

ARISTOTLE
(384-322 BC) Greek. Philosopher

So if we practice, practice, practice, this good habit will make us better each time. When I was a little girl my friend's Grandmother would say, "Good, better, best, never let it rest, until your good is better and your better is best." (I like it.)

Don't forget the flip side of this. If you practice bad things you'll get better at them too!

What a curious phenomenon it is that you can get men to die for the liberty of the world who will not make the little sacrifice that is needed to free themselves from their own individual bondage.

BRUCE BARTON
(1886-1967) American. Author, Advertising Executive

Did you ever notice that when you're with a group of people who are excited about doing something you feel more excited, more so than if you were doing the same thing by yourself?

Men and women will fight in war to preserve our freedoms, but have a difficult time freeing themselves from the things that cause a war in their own lives; things like drugs or alcohol.

One explanation for this is that as a group there is strength in numbers. You've got to be the one who gets the bad things out of your life, all by yourself. You can get support and encouragement from others but ultimately you have to do it all by your lonesome.

My niece Amanda says, "Get it in gear and don't forget to shift!" You have to have faith and believe in yourself and know you can do anything you set your mind to! You have to be willing to take that next step up to reach the stars. That's why we put it into high gear!

thoughts....

Happiness

Life is made up not of great sacrifices or duties,
but of the little things, in which smiles and
kindness and small obligations, given
habitually are what win and preserve
the heart and secure comfort.

HUMPHRY DAVY
(1778-1829) English. Scientist

The greatest men in all ages have been lovers
of their kind. All true leaders of men have it.
Faith in men and regard for men are
unfailing marks of true greatness.

RALPH WALDO EMERSON
(1803-1882) American. Essayist, Poet

The talent of success is nothing more than doing what you can do well, and doing well whatever you do...

HENRY WADSWORTH LONGFELLOW
(1807-1882) American. Poet

Success doesn't mean being the absolute best, success means *doing* your absolute best. Do your best and angels can do no better.

Another way to measure success is if you are working on your goals and making them happen. That's when you reach the winner's circle.

No one can become rich without enriching others. Anyone who adds to prosperity must prosper in return.

ALEXANDER ORNDORFF
(unavailable)

No man who continues to add something to the material, intellectual, and moral well-being of the place in which he lives is left long without proper reward.

BOOKER T. WASHINGTON
(1856-1915) American. Educator

Enjoy your own life without comparing it with that of another.

MARIE J. G. CONDORCET
(1743-1794) French. Philosopher, Political Leader, Mathematician

We are usually the most unhappy when we compare ourselves to other people.

Try to watch and learn from other people, but don't compare. We are all different people with many different thoughts and ideals. Be yourself, it's the only person you really can be!

Quotes for Kids

Of the blessings set before you, make your choice and be content.

SAMUEL JOHNSON
(1709-1784) English. Writer, Lexicographer

You can see the blessings around you if you are content. But if you are so busy blowin' and goin', you won't have time to see the cool things that are happening all around you. Make the decision to be satisfied with what you have.

This doesn't mean you shouldn't challenge yourself to see what you can do, or stop learning. It just means relax a little bit. I've heard it said this way - be content with what you have, while in pursuit of what you want. Yeah! That's the ticket!

There are two things to aim at in life: first, to get what you want; and, after that, to enjoy it. Only the wisest of mankind achieve the second.

LOGAN PEARSALL SMITH
(1865-1946) American. Essayist

If any man seeks for greatness, let him forget greatness and ask for truth, and he will find both.

HORACE MANN
(1796-1859) American. Educator

Search for answers in life. Search for the truth. There are some things that happen in this world that you and I will never be able to understand, but keep trying.

Knowing the truth about something can help you to understand why things happen the way they do or why some people feel the way they do. It's like adding two plus two together and coming up with four instead of eleven. It all adds up! It won't be so frustrating. You can go forward from here.

A joyful heart is good medicine, but a broken spirit dries up the bones.

PROVERBS 17:22

When it comes to the important things in life, laughter is one of them, because when we're laughin' we're livin'.

The human body is a fantastic machine. It is so well made that it even knows how to relieve itself of stress. The illustrator of this book, Dan Holt, Ph.D., explained it to me this way. Laughter from positive humor releases hormones in the body that are natural anti-depressants. These very same hormones work with the immune system to fight disease. So make sure you can laugh at yourself and with others, it will keep you healthier and you'll get laugh-lines instead of wrinkles.

Stress and humor must exist in order to create the dynamic force that propels the human animal. It is learning to accept both and utilize both, that people are able to advance beyond the fear of living and find the joy of life.

DAN G. HOLT, PH.D.
(November-2060 +/-) American. Extraordinary Guy

Learn

Tomorrow is the most important thing in life.
Comes to us at midnight very clean. It's perfect
when it arrives and puts itself in our hands.
It hopes we've learned something from
yesterday.

JOHN WAYNE
(1907-1979) American. Actor

Bad times have a scientific value. These are occasions a good learner would not miss.

RALPH WALDO EMERSON
(1803-1882) American. Essayist, Poet, Philosopher

Sometimes when bad things happen we feel sad or angry. But if you can say to yourself "things could be a lot worse," it will make you feel better.

Things happen for a reason. Most of the time the reason is to teach us something so we can help somebody else when they are having a rough time.

Bad times help us to remember the good times. If we would not have the bad times we would not appreciate what we have. Someday you might get hurt playing a sport and have to sit on the bench and watch everybody else play without you. Now you realize how much you've taken it for granted because you want to be out there too.

All our progress is an unfolding, like the vegetable bud.
You have first an instinct, then an opinion,
then a knowledge.

RALPH WALDO EMERSON
(1803-1882) American. Essayist, Poet, Philosopher

Let's say you want to learn how to in-line skate. Your instinct is desire; the natural force that says, "I want to."

You must believe you can learn how to skate. If your opinion is you can't learn, guess what - you never will!

Get all the information you can about in-line skating. With this knowledge you can actually start to practice, and when you practice you learn. (If you want to really be good, get skates and the gear too!)

When instinct, opinion and knowledge are all working together in a positive way, you will be skating down the street, in style. Life is good!

If a man empties all he knows into his head no one can take it away from him. An investment in knowledge always pays the best interest.

BENJAMIN FRANKLIN
(1706-1790) American. Printer, Author, Diplomat, Philosopher, Scientist

Some things like your money and other material things can be taken away from you. The things you've learned stay in your head and can't be stolen from you.

Some of the best rewards in life come from learning. Think about how good you feel when you get a good grade in school... YES!

A man learns little from victory; much from defeat.
CHINESE PROVERB

You can learn so much from your mistakes.
I guess this is because it's frustrating when you
make a mistake:

Like when you left your science book at your
friend's house and you had to go back and get it,
riding your bike barefoot, four miles in the pouring
rain, uphill both ways, just so you could finish studying
for Mrs. Proton's test the next day!

The good
news is you
can learn from
other people's
mistakes too!
That way you
won't make the
same mistakes that
they've made.
Just watch and learn.

*The great accomplishments of man have resulted
from the transmission of ideas and enthusiasm.*

THOMAS J. WATSON
(1874-1956) American. Industrialist

Just think what kind of a world we would live in
if we didn't follow through with our ideas and use our
creativity. We would still be writing our letters with a
feather pen instead of using a computer.

In 1949, while Mr. Watson
was chairman of the board, he
turned IBM Corporation into
a multi-million dollar
business. That's what
I call enthusiasm!

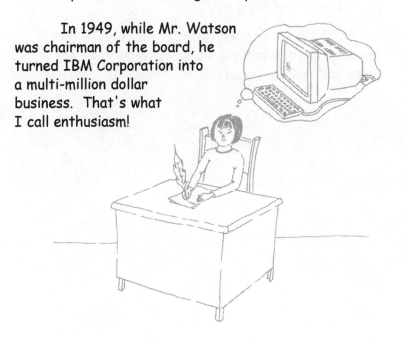

Vigor is contagious; and whatever makes us either think or feel strongly adds to our power and enlarges our field of action.

RALPH WALDO EMERSON
(1803-1882) American. Essayist, Poet

It's the excitement you feel when your team is winning and the crowd is going wild! It's why schools have Pep Rallies with screaming cheerleaders just before "the big game!"

The more excited you feel about something, the more determined you're going to be to go out there and make it happen!

Anyone who stops learning is old, whether this happens to be twenty or eighty. Anyone who keeps learning not only remains young but also becomes constantly more valuable.

HARVEY ULLMAN
(unavailable)

Some people say, learn something new everyday. I heard a pastor's wife once phrase it this way, "I didn't know that - I've learned something new, I'll live 'til midnight." I liked what she said, so I say the same thing when someone teaches me something new. It's like an incentive to those of us who want to live at least until midnight!

If you start working as a dishwasher in a restaurant and you gradually learn how to cook, operate the cash register, serve and host, you will be a more valuable employee than if you were to only wash dishes. Countless managers and business owners have worked their way up this way.

The more we learn today, the more we will be able to contribute to our tomorrows. So much stimulation is happening when you are learning. You feel alive! If you watch closely, I'll bet you can see yourself grow!

It is not a question of how much a man knows, but what use he makes of what he knows. Not a question of what he had acquired and how he has been trained, but of what he is and what he can do.

J. G. HOLLAND
(unavailable)

Back to the basics. You can have all the knowledge and ability but unless you apply what you know you won't go anywhere.

For instance: a new doctor has just completed his medical training and has the opportunity to work with an established doctor. Everything is all set to go. But, if the new doctor doesn't apply his skills, doesn't work to get new patients and decides to do nothing, all the things he knows will never be used. If you don't use it you lose it, you won't remember it. All that education goes down the drain!

If you apply yourself there is no limit to what you can do. Remember the only thing stopping you is you!

What we have to learn to do, we learn by doing.

ARISTOTLE
(384-322 BC) Greek. Philosopher, Scientist

Practice, practice, practice! I know you've heard it a million times before but, if you're ever gonna get any better at what you are doing now, it's the only thing that will work. The better you get at something the more confidence you get too!

Our grand business is undoubtedly, not to see what lies dimly at a distance but to do what lies clearly on hand.

THOMAS CARLYLE
(1795-1881) Scottish. Essayist, Historian

What you do now determines what you'll do and have in the future. Work with what you have and prepare for what you can reach in the distance.

That tree is very old, but I never saw prettier blossoms on it than it now bears. That tree grows new wood each year, like the apple tree, I try to grow a little new wood each year.

HENRY WADSWORTH LONGFELLOW
(1807-1882) American. Poet

Have you ever noticed the kind of personality that comes along with the person who always wants to learn new things? They are energetic and full of life. They don't want to miss a thing. If we keep trying to learn new things throughout our lives no matter how old we get, we will carry with us that same excitement and love for life. It shows!

Love and *Kindness*

Love is the most important ingredient of
success. Without it, our life echoes emptiness.
With it, our life vibrates warmth and meaning.
Even in hardship, love shines through.
Therefore, search for love. Once we have
learned to love, we will have learned to live.

UNKNOWN

Love

Love and kindness are action words. First do the "action" (the nice thing) and then the good feelings will come.

Say someone you love is working really hard in the yard. Wow, he looks thirsty, so you take him a tall glass of ice water. When he says thank you, doesn't it make you feel glad you brought the drink? Absolutely!

ACTS OF LOVE IN MOTION:
Working in the yard shows he cares.
You show your love by bringing the water.

See, you've got to do the act first, then the feelings come. KEEP THE ACTS COMING! It doesn't have to be someone you love, but it is a great place to start. Random acts of kindness work great on neighbors and friends (potential friends too)!

The opposite is true too. If you do mean things, mean and nasty feelings follow. Absolutely!

Love is not conditional on the acts, you need to accept and love people for who they are. Showing your love helps the feelings grow!

Love in its true form is not jealous or angry and does not expect anything in return.

Pure love accepts you for who and what you are, unconditionally, without any strings attached.

The warmth, peace and contentment that this kind of love brings cannot be accurately described.

Only the very fortunate feel it and recognize it.

It is God's most precious gift to us.
It is awesome!

What Goes Around Comes Around

How much effort does is take to give the people near you respect, consideration and love? Not much at all, but it is priceless to the people who are receiving your kindness.

Make a conscious effort to give more than you receive. Leave things a little better than you found them. Like if you borrow someone's hockey stick, clean it before you give it back, even if it was full of mud when you got it. (Maybe he didn't have time to clean it for you.) It only takes a little extra effort to do the right thing. It's another way of saying thank you very much for letting me use your hockey stick. It shows you're a good person.

Not everybody is going to treat you the same way, but don't let this stop you. The people who are the most unkind are usually the ones who need to see and feel your goodness the most.

More About Love

There is a famous poem that talks about love, setting it free, and if it comes back to you it's yours, and if it doesn't it wasn't meant to be.

Yes you must set love free, but if you don't give love any nurturing at all, it will fly so far away that it will never come back.

Love and relationships are like a garden. They take a lot of work, planting, weeding, watering, and most of the time one person does more work than the other person does. It should not be a chore; it should be something that you enjoy doing. The size of your garden will depend on how hard you work at it!

Kindness is the golden chain by which society is bound together.

JOHANN WOLFGANG VON GOETHE
(1749-1832) German. Poet, dramatist, Novelist, Scientist

When you are nice to other people and they are nice to you, that is kindness. It gives you a warm happy feeling and makes us feel close to each other.

The next time you enter a store hold the door open for the other person coming in. Some people will say thank you (usually the ones with their hands full), others will just walk right in, this is human nature. It feels good to just be nice without expecting anything in return.

Dad always said, "It's nice to be nice" and "Never take more than you give."

If I put you first and you put me first, no one will ever be second.

LISA MEYER

If I am thinking of your needs and you are thinking about mine, there's no need to be selfish or think only of ourselves. All the bases are covered. You give love, you get love.

When we are thinking only about ourselves it's like closing the blinds and blocking the warm sunlight from shining in.

*You can never do a kindness too soon for you
never know how soon will be too late.*

RALPH WALDO EMERSON
(1803-1882) American. Essayist, Poet, Philosopher

Do the nice things for the special people in your
life today. You don't know how many tomorrows you
have. Life is short. We have to plan for tomorrow
and live for today.

One of my favorite things to do is to drop in on
my Aunt Arlene at lunchtime with a pizza. It lets her
know I appreciate all she does and has done for me.
How do you show someone you care? There are lots of
little things that mean so much. Try a note, or a quick
phone call. And if you know their favorite little
something, get it for them. It will make both of you
feel so happy when you give it to them!

Nothing is ever lost by courtesy. It is the cheapest of
the pleasures; it costs nothing and conveys much.
It pleases him who gives and him who receives,
and thus, like mercy, is twice blessed.

ERASTUS WIMAN
(Unavailable)

You can only win by being polite. It tells so
much about who you are. It doesn't cost any money
and you get big returns on your investment of
kindness. You know the feeling, like when people do
nice things for you!

Get not your friends by bare compliments, but
by giving them sensible tokens of your love.

SOCRATES
(470?-399? BC) Greek. Philosopher

When you tell a friend "Hey I like your shirt,"
that's a nice thing to do. But when you help a friend,
it shows you care. It's called "acts of love," being a
friend.

P.S. This works great on family members too!

He that does good to another, does good also to himself,
not only in the consequences, but in the very act; for the
consequence of well doing is, in itself, ample reward.

SENECA
(4? BC-AD 65) Roman. Philosopher, Dramatist, Statesman

You give little when you give of your possessions.
It is when you give of yourself that you truly give.

KAHLIL GIBRAN
(1883-1931) American. Poet, Artist

Try to be a more giving person. You will be amazed at how great it feels to do nice things for other people. Honest! If you meet someone who doesn't seem to be too nice, be nice anyway. Maybe they have a good reason for being cranky (sometimes it's just a bad day). It will show that you are a nice person, and that you've got character!

We make a living by what we get, but we make a life by what we give.

WINSTON CHURCHHILL
(1874-1965) Great Britain. Statesman

Give what you have. To some it may be better than you dare think.

HENRY WADSWORTH LONGFELLOW
(1807-1882) American. Poet

So you may think that what you have to give may not be of any value to anyone else? How do you know that? Why do you think that? You never know until you ask or try to help. For all you know the other person could be secretly admiring you and wish they could be more like you.

Maybe there is someone who would really like to have that broken down old bike of yours, because it's in a whole lot better shape than the one they have now.

One man's junk is another man's treasure. This is why yard sales and flea markets are so popular!

Opportunity

Always hold fast to the present. Every
situation, indeed every moment, is of
infinite value, for it is the representative
of a whole eternity.

JOHANN WOLFGANG VON GOETHE
(1749-1832) German. Poet, Dramatist, Novelist, Scientist

CARPE DIEM! SEIZE THE DAY!

My country owes me nothing. It gave me as it gives every boy and girl, a chance. It gave me schooling, independence of action, opportunity for service and honor. In no other land could a boy from a country village without inheritance or influential friends look forward with unbound hope.

HERBERT HOOVER
(1874-1964) American. The 31st President of the United States

Do you really know what an incredible country we live in? How can you appreciate all that we have unless you have been to other countries yourself? Well you can read about them. Or listen to the stories of other people who have risked their lives just to be an American.

Take a look around you, visit the library (the state libraries are awesome) or picnic at a state park. There are so many things we take for granted every day. No other country gives their people as many privileges as ours does. Be the one who doesn't take our country and our freedoms for granted. See it! Love it! Live it!

To improve the golden moments of opportunity, and catch the good that is within our reach, is the great art of life.

SAMUEL JOHNSON
(1709-1784) English. Writer, Lexicographer (helps to write dictionaries)

Opportunities are all around us. You have to be alert and ready when opportunity comes. Most times it is right in front of us! There is a story about an African farmer who sold his land and went searching for diamonds. The new owner of the farm started digging for diamonds and found one of the richest diamond mines ever discovered in the world.

Start digging! Don't sell out until you are sure all of the diamonds are found. Then go looking for some more or make your own!

It is in men as it is in soils where sometimes there is a vein of gold which the owner knows not of.

JONATHAN SWIFT
(1667-1745) Anglo-Irish. Satirist, Political Pamphleteer (he made pamphlets)

A wise man will make more opportunities than he finds.

BACON
(unavailable)

Some people see things as problems; others see them as learning experiences or opportunities.

If you change your thinking about things soon you will see things in a positive way. Like when "life brings you lemons make lemonade."

A pessimist is one who makes difficulties of his opportunities; an optimist makes opportunities of his difficulties.

REGINALD B. MANSELL
(unavailable)

My friend Bonnie Kaye sent me a note one day about optimism and it said, "Two men looked out from prison bars: one saw the mud, the other the stars." If you can look out the window and look up instead of looking down, I'd say you are making the best of a bad situation. And if you think about it why would you look at the mud anyway? The stars will be as bright as you make them! Shine on, oh brave and wonderful one!

Problem Solving

*The heart of all problems, whether economic,
political, or social, is a human heart.*

CHARLES EDWARDS
(unavailable)

The scientific way of solving a problem:

1) Write the problem down on paper. See it clearly.

2) List the things that stand in the way of solving it.

3) List other people and sources that might be able to help you with the problem.

4) List as many solutions to the problem as possible. (This one takes time.)

5) Try to see the results of each possible solution.

6) Pick the solution that seems best to you. Try it long enough to see if it works. If it doesn't, choose another solution from the list.

The next time you've got troubles, try this formula, it works for me!

All problems become smaller if, instead of indulging in them, we confront them. Touch a thistle timidly and it pricks you; grasp it boldly, and the spines crumble.

WILLIAM S. HALSEY
(unavailable)

Pretend the problem is like a ball coming towards you, the harder you work at kicking it, the farther it goes away.

Some problems are not so simple and they don't just go away by themselves. You have to find the right solution. Sometimes you'll need help, don't be afraid to ask for it!

My Dad used to say, "All problems have an answer, you just have to find the answer, that's all." He was right!

Don't accept superficial solutions to difficult problems.

BERTRAND RUSSELL
(1872-1970) British. Philosopher, Mathematician, Nobel Laureate

If you take the easy way out you better look out, because the problem will probably come back right where it started from.

What if you have bubble gum stuck to the bottom of your shoe and you don't take the time to get it all off. You will be stuck with it until you do. Take care of the problem, the right way, the first time! It will help keep you out of sticky situations.

Respect

You cannot possess love without respect.
Respect and love have an inseparable union,
one of acceptance, understanding and honor.
They cannot walk alone; if they try to they
will stumble and fall. Together they dance,
and the music of life is sweet.

LISA MEYER

Respect

Michael Bolton sings a song that says, "You can conquer the world but it's never enough because you ain't got nothin' if you ain't got love." This is so true. And, you ain't got nothin' if you ain't got respect! Respect is such a huge word. If you don't have respect for other things, other people and yourself, you cannot possibly be truly happy.

If you have a bike and you don't keep it clean, or if you don't care if it gets all scratched up it means you don't have respect. It shows you are disrespectful. This is not a good thing.

If you are thoughtful, considerate and don't talk in a harsh way to someone, that's respect. Even if they are not showing you respect, it means that you have respect for yourself by not being harsh to them (you can be firm, not harsh). Remember it's usually not worth it to let people get you upset.

Self-respect is so important because if you don't have respect for yourself, others can't respect you either. Do you see how this can be true?

Do you see how catastrophic your life will be if you don't have respect? If you don't care about anybody or anything you can't care about yourself either.

I once read a short verse that said very simply, indifference is the absence of love.

I quietly say these words to anyone whenever I hear them say, "I don't care." It means if you don't care about something, then you don't love it. I want them to think about what they've just said. Maybe they really do care but they just don't know how to show it. I hope so. Some people think they are in love, but if they are disrespectful it's impossible to truly love other people or themselves.

It is possible to show respect for someone that you don't love. Like respect for a teacher, police officer or fire fighter. And, as strange as it may seem you can dislike a person for whatever reason, and still have respect for them. Because you can honor, value and recognize them for the job they do, just as you would a U.S. Soldier.

So, how do you get respect you ask? Well if your mother or your father doesn't drill it into your head as a child like mine has, it's tough. It's like any of the other stuff in life we have to learn. You have to learn it as you are growing up, or as an adult you have to want to learn it. Get started by studying the things in this book. Read it again and again until the message becomes clear and simple to you.

Respect and love walk together in a relationship. You can't have love without respect. It would be like having a CD player without the CD; it would be useless, you have nothing. But, the two together WOW! Now you have something awesome! So crank up the volume, enjoy the music of life, and DANCE! It's what makes it worthwhile.

thoughts....

Thinking

Sooner or later she begins to think; and no man knows what then she may discover.

EDWIN A. ROBINSON
(1869-1935) American. Poet, three-time Pulitzer Prize winner

Some men see things as they are and say why; I dream things that never were and say why not?

GEORGE BERNARD SHAW
(1859-1950) English. Dramatist, Critic

*Thinking is the hardest work there is, which is the
probable reason why so few people engage in it.*

HENRY FORD
(1863-1947) American. Industrialist

Your mind is the world's most precious
resource. Or at least you should think of it that way.
Yet the average person only uses about 10% of it,
that's it!

There is nothing better than to get a great idea
and then act on it. Just like me writing this book.

But the idea has to come first. So be creative
with your thoughts, and listen to other people's
thoughts too; usually one good thought leads to
another.

All life is an experiment. The more experiments you make the better.

RALPH WALDO EMERSON
(1803-1882) American. Essayist, Poet, Philosopher

Think about scientists. They are always testing their ideas and making new discoveries.

Be the scientist of your life. Don't be afraid to try new things that you think would be cool because you never know, it just may turn out the way you hope it will. But, if it doesn't don't give up. You'll learn from your mistakes.

Few moments are more pleasing than those in which the mind is concerting measures for a new undertaking.

SAMUEL JOHNSON
(1709-1784) English. Writer, Lexicographer (helps to make dictionaries)

It is good to rub and polish our brain against that of others.

MONTAIGNE
(1533- 1592) French. Writer

Do you know what goes on in all those business meetings? Well you do now; they are rubbing and polishing their heads against one another! That's where all those cool ideas come from like, "How will we put the toothpaste in the tube?" and the wonder of all wonders, "How in the heck do those airplanes fly?"

So start rubbing heads with some people. Make sure they know a bit more than you do or you won't learn anything. That's what we're after, to be big and smart, right? Maybe after your meeting your airplane will fly higher, faster and longer!

Quotes for Kids

When we see men of worth, we should think of becoming like them; when we see men of a contrary character, we should turn inward and examine ourselves.

CONFUCIUS
Chinese. Philosopher

I am a people watcher! (Older ladies in particular.) I think it is really neat to see what other people are doing with their lives. I try to learn how they have been able to achieve so many things in their lives. You can really learn a lot by watching other people. I ask myself, what sacrifices am I willing to make to reach achievement? Or what can I do to make sure my life doesn't end up unproductive?

I can remember when I worked as a waitress and some ladies were very kind and gracious, and I would think to myself, someday you will be sitting at the table and not serving it and you remember this day and be extra polite and gracious too! That day has come. I have learned a lot from strangers. I can honestly say I have kept my promise to myself.

Thinking

Think, think, think! Concentrate, concentrate, concentrate! Don't limit yourself. Don't let other people tell you "You can't do that" without asking "Why not?" Listen to their answer, then decide for yourself what you can't do, or find another way to do it. So many people lose out on some really cool things just because someone told them they couldn't do it. When my daughter Christi uses the word can't I say, "Oh but you can, watch this."

About two weeks before my Aunt Sandie's fiftieth birthday (December 19), she decided she would like to have a nice party rather than gifts. My Aunt Sandie is also one of my best friends. Because she means so much to me, I had to make this happen. My family members thought it was impossible to find a banquet room because it was so close to Christmas, but not "ole deputy dog" (that's what my friend Bonnie Kaye calls me). I made some phone calls and found the perfect spot. It was so perfect we used it for an engagement party in April.

So, you can be a "deputy dog" and make things happen or you can be the flea on the dog and wonder "what's happening?" It's all up to you!

All mankind is divided into three classes: those that are immovable, those that are movable, and those that move.

BENJAMIN FRANKLIN
(1706-1790) American. Printer, Author, Diplomat, Philosopher, Scientist

If you are immovable you don't want to go anywhere. You just won't move.

If you are moveable you are a follower. You want to go some place but you're just not sure how to get there.

If you are one of those that move then you are a leader.

Which one are you? Which one do you want to be?

About the Author

This book isn't really just my book. It's pieces of everyone who has ever touched my life. All those people who've sensed that I was ready to listen and then shared their thoughts and what they believe in. Words and thoughts of inspiration that came from someone before them. This is one of the ways we pass things down from one generation to the next. It is a far more valuable inheritance than the family silver, don't you think?

I once met a young man by the name of Nate who absolutely overwhelmed me by his musical talents and determination. I told him if life were a box of chocolates, he would not be the one you would take a bite of and then put back in the box, but he would be the reason to buy the box in the first place. It pleased him. I can't wait to watch him fly. You see you never know what you might say or do that will have an impact on someone for the rest of their life. Think about the number of times you may have done the very same thing.

Would it really matter to you if I had a degree? Would it make a difference to you if I had the credentials like a Ph.D.? Well I must tell you I have no formal degree. But I am a scholar. The learning wheel of life is always turning my thoughts. How does it work? Why did he/she do that? What is the best way to do this? These are questions I repeatedly ask myself. I am a thinker. Emerson said, "Beware when the great God lets loose a thinker on his planet." I like Emerson's thinking. Maybe he would have liked mine too!

Maybe Mr. Emerson would have liked some of my thoughts about life. I believe so much in being a happy person and sharing that happiness wherever I can. When we're laughin' we're livin'! I talk to strangers. My best friends once were strangers to me. Think about where we all would be if we never talked to strangers. I try not to take things and people for granted, and to be thankful for what I have. I realize that contentment can bring peace. I know a good definition for luck, it's when preparedness meets opportunity. I don't know the definition of a coincidence. Is there really such a thing? I believe in God, the power of love, and I believe in myself.

God has cleared the path for me to write this book, all the doors have flown open. For those of you who listen and walk along your own faith journey, you know what I'm talking about. I've prayed all the way that I've made the right decisions, for His words to come through me, onto the paper, and into your heart. Use it to shine through your life and into the lives of others. That's truly what life is all about!

Lisa Meyer is available for author visits and a variety of workshop/presentations. For information, contact:

P.O. Box 764
Hershey, PA 17033
reachlisa@earthlink.net
1.888.70REACH
www.quotesforkids.com

Index

Quotes for Kids

Sources

Every effort has been made to appropriately credit the copyright owners of material quoted in this reference. If any sources have not been sufficiently credited, please contact the publisher and efforts will be made to correct in subsequent printings.

Gale's Quotations Who Said What ©1995 Gale Research Inc.

This is Earl Nightingale, Earl Nightingale ©1969 Pub. Doubleday Ferguson

The Treasure Chest, Charles L. Wallis ©1965 by Charles L. Wallis, Published by Harper Collins ©1995 by HarperCollins Publishers, Inc.

Treasury of Familiar Quotations Edited & Published by Averel books © 1955, 1963 by Ottenheimer Publishers, Inc.

Words of Wisdom; More Good Advice, Compiled and Edited by William Safire and Leonard Safir ©1989 Published by Simon & Schuster N.Y.

Contributors

Schaeffer & Associates Printing - *pre-press, production*
Jane Miller & Associates - *editing, proofing*
Digital Imaging Solutions Corporation (D.I.S.C.)
Robert Howard Photography

Ordering Information

Available Nationally: Local Bookstores, Educators, Contact Your Local Distributor or Please Send Check or Money Order To:

Reach Press ❧ P.O. Box 764 ❧ Hershey, PA 17033

Price: $13.95 each - PA residents add 6% sales tax ($.84) per book.
Shipping: $2.50 for the first book $.50 for each additional book.

To ensure proper delivery, please be sure to include the ship to address in correspondence .

Please allow 2-3 weeks for delivery
Yes! Quantity Discounts Yes! Fund Raising

Inquiries and Presentation Information Contact:
1-888-70REACH (1-888-707-3224) reachlisa@earthlink.net

www.quotesforkids.com